BEYOND RED ROCKS

JOHN

BEYOND RED ROCKS

TESH

making your dreams a reality

TYNDALE HOUSE PUBLISHERS INC., WHEATON, ILLINOIS

This book is dedicated to my wife, Connie.
Without her support, love, and guidance, I would never have had the courage
to tackle either of the Red Rocks concerts. Connie was with me for the risk,
the hard work, and the prayer. She will always have "my back" and my heart.
It's an honor to call her my partner.

Visit Tyndale's exciting Web site at www.tyndale.com

www.tesh.com

Cover photograph of John Tesh © 2004 by Charles William Bush. All rights reserved.
Cover photograph of Red Rocks © 2003 Kevin Burke. All rights reserved.
Interior photo insets and portraits of John Tesh: pp. 6, 82-83 © 2004 by Charles William Bush. All rights reserved. Interior photographs: pp. 12-13, 21, 31, 41, 51, 71, 81, 91 © 2004 by Carrie Fedewa. All rights reserved. Interior photographs: pp. 16,19, 22-23, 26, 29, 32-33, 36, 39, 42-43, 46, 49, 52-53, 59, 61, 76, 89 © 2003 Kevin Burke. All rights reserved. Interior photographs: pp. 62-63, 66, 72-73, 79, 86 © 1993 by Charles William Bush. All rights reserved. Interior photographs: pp. 69, 95 Courtesy of Michael Goldman.

Designed by Lucas A. Daab
Edited by Erin Keeley Marshall
Unless otherwise indicated, Scripture quotations are taken from the *Holy Bible*, New Living Translation, copyright © 1996. Used by permission of Tyndale House Publishers, Inc., Wheaton, Illinois 60189.
All rights reserved.
Scripture quotations marked NIV are taken from the *Holy Bible*, New International Version®. NIV®.
Copyright © 1973, 1978, 1984 by International Bible Society. Used by permission of Zondervan Publishing House. All rights reserved.
Printed in the United States of America
ISBN 0-8423-6570-2

08	07	06	05	04
5	4	3	2	1

TABLE OF CONTENTS

A NOTE TO READERS

Sail away from the safe harbor. Catch the trade winds in your sails.
Explore. Dream. Discover.

—

MARK TWAIN

I have always believed in giving all I've got to pursue my dreams. Not many experiences compare with the sense of fulfillment that comes from taking a leap of faith and risking the loss of something familiar for the opportunity of something greater. The past decade of my life not only has witnessed the culmination of a lifelong desire to be a full-time musician but also has challenged and grown me in ways I did not expect.

The realization of my dream began the night I played my first concert at the Red Rocks Amphitheatre near Denver,

Colorado. At that point I was thrilled to be recording music. But I didn't know back then the direction my new career would take.

Several years ago I was introduced to a new genre of music known as praise and worship. I started playing with the worship team at church, and before long my band was performing church concerts all over the country.

As time went on, I began mixing more spiritually based songs in nearly every concert, most of which were in secular venues. Nevertheless, the spiritual emphasis soon became an integral part of my overall performance.

So convinced was I of the transforming power of praise and worship music that I decided to return to Red Rocks in October 2003 for a full-blown worship concert.

It was awesome to revisit the scene of the first major turning point in my musical career. This time, however, my intent was not to launch a new career; it was to say thank you to the one who makes it all possible. Today, my top priority is to love God with a pure love and to do what he wants me to do with pure motives.

I never planned for my life to happen the way it has. Looking back, it's amazing to see how everything has come together to get me where I am today. I have been a reporter, a television personality, a radio-show host, a musician, and a composer, as well as a husband, father, and stepdad. I'm not a teacher, preacher, or coach; I have no ordination papers and no doctoral attributions behind my name. In fact, I'm not an expert on much of anything, except dreaming big and being willing to take a risk.

My life has always been about risk—stepping out of my

comfort zone. Along the way I have risked humiliation, the derisive laughter of my peers, and setbacks in my career. I have risked my emotional security and my fragile self-image. But to me, the risk was worth it.

The great American novelist Mark Twain once said, "Twenty years from now you will be more disappointed by the things you didn't do than by the ones you did do." When all is said and done, I don't ever want to sit back, review my life, and wonder what might have been.

Through it all—the good, the bad, and the ugly—I have tried to remain open to the inner promptings of God. No matter how well I performed or how badly I messed up, my life has remained in a positive, forward motion under his direction. I often stumbled in the dark, and when I reached out for help, God's hand was there to pick me up, brush me off, and get me going again. That same hand waits to help you when you stumble too. You need only reach out and accept it.

In the next few chapters I'd like to share with you some key truths my Red Rocks journey taught me about dreams, knowing my purpose in life, living with passion, taking risks, moving forward in faith, acting courageously, finding fulfillment, and leaving behind a legacy. I hope that after reading these pages you will be convinced that, with God as your conductor, your life can become a symphony of joy and fulfillment. And I hope you will catch the sense of adventure that awaits you as you dare to follow your dreams and do what others say can't or shouldn't be done.

To echo Twain, the time has come to "Sail away from the safe harbor. Catch the trade winds in your sails.

Explore. Dream. Discover."

DREAM

All people dream, but not equally. . . .
The dreamers of the day are dangerous people,
for they dream their dreams with open eyes,
and make them come true.

—

T. E. LAWRENCE

Just dreaming about nice things is meaningless;
it is like chasing the wind.

—

ECCLESIASTES 6:9

In quiet moments of solitude, when your innermost desires break through into conscious thought, where do your hopes take you? If you were freed from all boundaries and limitations, what is the one goal you would give almost anything to attain, the achievement that makes your pulse race with excitement and fear? We all have great God-given dreams buried within. Those dreams require a leap of faith, but as long as they remain untapped we will always have a sense of frustration and futility. Regardless of our other successes, something is missing.

Explaining away why those dreams remain unfulfilled becomes second nature. How easy and comfortable it is to rattle off rote responses to stuff the dream back down. After all, the big unknowns outside our comfort zone can seem terrifying . . . even irresponsibly unreliable.

But what is the cost? Stepping out in faith or reaching the end of your life with regrets—wishing you had taken your dream more seriously?

 My dream was to perform my music in front of a live audience at the magnificent Red Rocks Amphitheatre near Denver, Colorado.

Ever since I was a child, music has been my passion. As an adult, I strived for success as a musician, performing on the small-scale stages of jazz clubs and local performing arts centers. From my first day on the set of *Entertainment Tonight,* I told the producers that my dream was to be a full-time musician. Although I was squeezing in my composing between announcing celebrity birthdays, my life's dream was to put together melodies that would lift people's spirits.

Yet I had never put myself in a position to really test my mettle. For years I resigned myself to a halfway pursuit, putting off the time when I would cross that invisible line of no return and find success or failure doing my heart's passion.

A nd you? What dreams have you put on the shelf? Likely you have a dream that seems impossible, but it continues to pique your imagination. You may have a spoken or imagined point of no return. Are you willing to settle for a life of What ifs?

Do whatever it takes to understand the desires deepest in your heart. It's possible they have been buried so long that they are difficult to recognize, but a little digging will unearth your dreams. Get away by yourself; take an overnight retreat or set aside a couple of hours when your mind can stop spinning from life's responsibilities long enough for you to hear your quietest inner thoughts.

Discover what dreams are uniquely yours.

Your hopes, dreams, and aspirations are legitimate. They are trying to take you airborne, above the clouds, above the storms, if you only let them.

—

WILLIAM JAMES

[Dream. Plan. Live.]

Sometimes dreams alter the course of an entire life.

—

JUDITH DUERK

[God created the dream.]

PURPOSE

One can never consent to creep
when one feels an impulse to soar.

—

HELEN KELLER

My purpose is to give life in all its fullness.

—

JOHN 10:10

God has built into our nature an uneasiness with the status quo. We know instinctively that we were created to do more than simply hang around waiting to die. We recognize that this world is not all there is for us, that we were designed for total commitment and eternal love. Simply put, we were designed by God for his purposes.

There is something deep within you that says, "I was built for better than what I am experiencing." That tension between being content in your life and sensing that there is more God wants you to do most likely will exist as long as you walk the earth.

If you're not careful, it can become extremely convenient to shelve your dreams while you busy yourself with the mundane chores of life—many good, necessary things, but not the stuff that most people's dreams are made of.

Ten years ago I did a concert at Red Rocks because I wanted to change my life. I wanted people to hear my music. I wanted it to be my experience. I wanted things to be better for me. Now, ten years later, I want to be useful. The difference between Red Rocks ten years ago and Red Rocks last summer is a matter of losing selfishness and having a greater purpose than myself.

When I was still working at *Entertainment Tonight,* people at church would say to me, "John, you're playing music in church, but you're also on a show that features Victoria's Secret models. I don't get it—which person are you?" That was a big question I had to ask myself. *Which person am I?*

I used to measure myself by my paycheck, and the ridiculous passion for money was burning me out. The moment I started recording worship music my record sales dropped 40 percent, but I was having 100 percent more fun. This is where I feel I can be most useful. I want people to say, "That's the guy who walked away from a seven-figure salary to follow his dream, and now he's playing worship songs."

Purpose made the difference.

It's time to break out of the status quo.

When God gives you a purpose, he wants you to pursue that goal. To neglect taking that purpose seriously is to cheat yourself, the world, and God.

Ask yourself each day whether you are living intentionally. Are you a vital participant in your own life? The recognition of purpose is like the glow of a fire's embers; with a breath of life, that glow builds to a strong, blazing fire that changes the conditions of its environment.

What makes your life glow?

Those who have attained things worth having in this world have worked while others idled, have persevered while others gave up in despair, have practiced . . . singleness of purpose.

—

GRENVILLE KLEISER

[Live on purpose.]

So I run straight to the goal with purpose in every step.

—

I CORINTHIANS 9:26

[Discover your God-given purpose.]

PASSION

If what you're working for really matters,
you'll give it all you've got.

—

NIDO QUBEIN

You must find a way to do what you love.
To enjoy your work . . . that is indeed a gift from God.

—

ECCLESIASTES 5:19

One of the keys to success is to find a way to do what you love. If you get paid for it, great—that's the icing on the cake. Truth is, if you are doing something you love, sooner or later the money often will follow. But what is most important is that you pour yourself into God-honoring work that you are absolutely passionate about.

Unfortunately, many people are not doing what they really want to do in life. They are trapped in a career they have little enthusiasm for, living in a situation they don't enjoy, and spinning their wheels in frustration, sacrificing their dreams in exchange for a regular paycheck.

Many would leave or quit . . . if it wasn't for the bills, the kids' college education, the health insurance that accompanies the paycheck, or some other perfectly logical reason for enduring another day of drudgery.

But if you want to feel good about yourself and be truly successful, you must find a way to do what you love. Even if nobody understands, even if it isn't financially lucrative, even if you don't get paid for it at all!

There's something about sitting behind a grand piano—never do I feel more connected to God. I think it's because I'm there in front of the dream that God gave me. Composing and performing music is my life's passion. It's what gets me up early in the morning and keeps me going long after my physical energy should have waned. When I was at *Entertainment Tonight,* I felt trapped. I loved doing the show, being a reporter, and being on television, but I had grown up wanting to be on stage, sitting behind a grand piano, and playing to a live audience—that was my real passion.

One night my wife and I were watching television and saw a concert at this place called Red Rocks. The bands were playing in the rain and fog, rocks filling the background. I thought, *That's the place! I want to be in that place, playing my music in front of a full orchestra.* We approached PBS about airing the concert, but they were less than enthused about the idea. There wasn't anybody behind me saying, "Yes, this is a great idea," other than my wife, Connie. But it didn't matter—the passion wouldn't let go.

How would you like to wake up tomorrow knowing you are going to spend the day doing something you really enjoy, something that excites you and brings joy to your life?

You know in your heart what your passion is—everybody does. What will it take to live it out? The only way to figure out what to do with your passion is to get alone in the presence of God. He created passion in the human heart, and he will reveal a plan to you.

Success is not the key to happiness. Happiness is the key to success.

If you love what you are doing, you will be successful.

—

ALBERT SCHWEITZER

[There is no true living without passion.]

Nobody cares if you can't dance well. Just get up and dance.
Great dancers are not great because of their technique,
they are great because of their passion.

—

MARTHA GRAHAM

[Ask God to ignite your passion for
whatever he wants you to do.]

RISK

Our lives improve only when we take chances—
and the first and most difficult risk we can take
is to be honest with ourselves.

—

WALTER ANDERSON

Show me the path where I should walk,
O Lord; point out the right road for me to follow.

—

PSALM 25:4

W hat is the difference between people who settle for a mediocre existence and those who live with passion and exuberance? I'm convinced it's the willingness to risk.

You were made to thrive. Giving in to the fear of taking risks makes for an unsatisfying life. When you dare to attempt a feat so far outside your comfort zone that your heart nearly bursts with excitement, something exhilarating happens. No longer can you be appeased by less meaningful things.

You know that sensation, don't you? The stomach flip that comes every time a new opportunity pops up in front of you. It's part excitement, part nausea as you wonder, *Do I dare to think I could actually do that?*

Maybe it's something that has never been done before. Or maybe it's something others have done millions of times, yet you have never tried it. The effect is the same: Fresh energy courses through you, and you wonder: *Can I risk it? What if I fail? Worse yet, what if I have to live the rest of my life knowing I had an opportunity but shrank from it because of my fears?*

If you have known any of those feelings—and which of us hasn't?—then you have an idea of my inner turmoil as I prepared for what was probably one of the most outlandish risks I have ever taken: performing my first live concert, complete with an eighty-piece symphony orchestra, at Red Rocks.

As I seriously began to consider that Herculean undertaking, question after question pummeled my heart and mind. *Can I play? Will people want to hear me? What if nobody shows up?*

But the drive was relentless. I wanted to do something huge to show I was serious about music. When I began praying about what I wanted to do with my life, it became very clear to me that I needed to leave television. Even if I wasn't successful at Red Rocks, I was going to have to throw myself out there and do what was in my heart—otherwise I might never have the opportunity again. It was so clear to me, but it wasn't clear to anybody else.

There's no denying it: Leaving your place of security and stepping out into the unknown to do something you truly believe you must do can be terrifying, especially if others around you don't agree or understand.

Those voices of doom will always lurk around your dreams: *Are you crazy? That's dangerous! Think about all you have to lose.* If you let them, they will freeze you in your tracks.

Here are a few battle plans. . . .

Realize that you will sometimes fail. At some point you will hit a wrong note, forget your next line, say the wrong thing, or make the wrong move. Consider this: Is the worst thing that could result from that failure bigger than the results if you succeed? Own the results of failure and the fear of it will diminish.

Know your material well. If you put yourself on the line to do something, it's worth doing with excellence.

Know when to laugh. Especially, know when to laugh at yourself. A smile in the face of adversity often defuses it.

Most important—*Keep your eyes on the prize.* Look straight ahead and fix your vision on what lies before you. Mark out a straight path for your feet, then stick to it.

[You have only one life; your time is now.]

Dare to live the life you have dreamed for yourself.
Go forward and make your dreams come true.

—

RALPH WALDO EMERSON

[Pray. Risk. Trust.]

FAITH

Live your beliefs
and you can turn the world around.

—

HENRY DAVID THOREAU

Taste and see that the Lord is good.
Oh, the joys of those who trust in him!

—

PSALM 34:8

Faith is the foundation on which everything else of lasting value must be built. It's the fuel that produces the courage to take a risk when the opportunity comes along.

Faith illuminates the stage of your heart and mind. You stand center stage with the one who created the universe and can bring true harmony to your soul. The one who created you, who knows you better than anyone else, and who longs for a relationship with you. If you have faith in Jesus, you aren't lost in the dark even when things happen that you don't understand. You can believe—know without the shadow of a doubt—that no matter how lost you may feel, a divine plan is at work.

If you keep your faith in God, you can rest in the fact that he is in charge. And if you choose to trust him, he will lead you on the best path for you.

As I prayed about my dream to perform at Red Rocks, the answer kept coming back that I needed to struggle with some questions. *What am I going to do? Where is my heart? And what am I going to do if things don't work out?* After all, I was in a really safe place, and I was making a lot of money.

Even so, my wife and I realized the concert would take more money than we had. But with her encouragement we stepped out in faith and mortgaged our home, and six months later there we were on stage with an eighty-piece orchestra, in front of a full house of ten thousand.

I had prayed for a year that this would be a huge television special that would launch my full-time music career. But God had me backing into another blessing.

Three songs into the concert of my dreams, it started pouring rain, and the orchestra walked offstage. *That's it,* I thought. *This is over. I'm going to lose my house. I'm a fool.* My brain scrambled for Scripture, and I came up with Philippians 4:12-13: "I have learned

the secret of being content in any and every situation. . . .
I can do everything through him who gives me strength" (NIV).

My featured violinist suggested we play anyway. Finally the
moon came out, and about two songs later, it stopped raining, the
orchestra came back, and we finished the concert.

The way we handled that three-song struggle in the rain was
the catalyst that got PBS to sign the show, and it ended up being
one of the most popular pledge specials on PBS. It also defined for
me how deep risk can be, how crucial faith is, and how important
it is to trust God.

With the assurance that your life is in God's hands, dare to do what you love, knowing that even if you make a wrong turn and find yourself in a dead end, God will continue to nudge you back in the right direction.

If you have faith, maintain your focus, and work hard, God will take you on a journey beyond anything you could do on your own. His plan may not be the same as the one you had, but it will be one that will work for your life.

Take the first step in faith.
You don't have to see the whole staircase, just take the first step.

—

DR. MARTIN LUTHER KING, JR.

[Believe the answer will come.]

With God everything is possible.

—

MATTHEW 19:26

[Partner with God
and accomplish the dream.]

COURAGE

The battle . . . is not to the strong alone;
it is to the vigilant, the active, the brave.

—

PATRICK HENRY

And we know that God causes everything
to work together for the good of those who love God
and are called according to his purpose for them.

—

ROMANS 8:28

W e don't need courage if we plan to maintain the status quo. With no changes, challenges, or unknowns facing us, there's really no threat to our comfort zone. However, attempting anything new invites opportunities to choose fight or flight. Aside from our self-inflicted battles of confidence, what are some "courage busters"?

Rejection and criticism are two. Rejection is always difficult to deal with, no matter how confident we are or how impervious we have become to other people's opinions. The good news is that rejection is rarely fatal and most messes can be cleaned up. God often takes circumstances we regard as our greatest failures or disappointments and uses them to bring about good in our lives.

Criticism is a close cousin of rejection. Nobody enjoys being criticized. Sometimes, though, we can learn from constructive criticism. The trick, of course, is to screen out the destructive comments while considering those that might yield a kernel of truth. As you pursue new adventures, the best thing you can do is to learn from your mistakes and move on. Each day will take you another step away from the pain of past disappointments. Before long you will be so invigorated, you will have renewed courage to take a risk again.

It's amazing how much we can be affected by the pessimism of others. If we let it get to us, fear grows and courage wanes.

As I've said, although my dream was clear to me, it wasn't clear to anybody else. In my Red Rocks quest, I dealt with my share of faltering courage. In addition to all the risks, I used to suffer from severe stage fright to the point that I would lose feeling in my hands. When I started touring, I was so nervous that I actually lost feeling in my left arm. So I learned more about the power of prayer.

Fear is a destroyer. Even now at my concerts, I tell people, "The only thing holding you back from following your heart is fear—whether it's fear of getting closer to God, fear of relationships, fear of going where your heart wants to go. . . ."

People ask me what I'm thinking about when I play the piano. In the beginning it was, "Am I going to make a mistake?" Now I'm just in constant prayer.

It's easier to steer a boat that is moving than one that is tied up at the dock. Don't give too much credence to the naysayers, those who are overly cautious and afraid to take a risk. That includes your own self-doubts. Instead, listen to the people who encourage you to venture out with courage and faith, to push away from the shore and see where your boat will go.

When rejection or criticism come your way—as they will sooner or later—sure, they will hurt. They may stagger you or even knock you down for a while. But don't allow them to destroy your dreams. Brush off your confidence and get back up. Consider your options and then begin moving in a direction that excites you.

Inspiration builds courage. While I was rehearsing for the concert, Connie sent me a picture of our new daughter, Prima, in her crib. The photo was inscribed with the words "Daddy, I miss you! Prima." I kept the photo and note on the piano throughout all our rehearsals to inspire me.

What inspires your courage?

[Courage is your choice.]

Strength and courage aren't always measured in medals
and victories. They are measured in the struggles they overcome.
The strongest people aren't always the people who win,
but the people who don't give up when they lose.

—

ASHLEY HODGESON

[Find courage through prayer.]

FULFILLMENT

To improve the golden moment of opportunity,
and catch the good that is within our reach,
is the great art of life.

—

SAMUEL JOHNSON

God, who began the good work within you,
will continue his work until it is finally finished
on that day when Christ Jesus comes back again.

—

PHILIPPIANS 1:6

Life cannot be lived fully if it is approached frivolously. To step out in faith with God into the unknown and to do something you believe in brings a fulfillment not found in less passionate hearts. There's a rare feeling of worth that comes only from valuing your dreams enough to do what it takes to nurture them to life.

One of the most awesome realities of fulfillment is that each of us finds it in different ways. We are created uniquely, with individual passions, temperaments, and talents. However, we have the same Creator, who knows each of us individually. He knows the best path for you as well as for me. Knowing him is the key to finding fulfillment. Begin there and see where he leads.

It's funny. Nothing in my life had suggested that Red Rocks could happen; yet, in some strange way, I knew that everything about my life had led me to that point. As hard as it was for me to believe, there I was, up on stage—a kid from Garden City, New York—there in the majestic, phenomenal natural beauty created by God. I wanted to give my best as a gift to God. And God worked to make the results into an awesome rhapsody!

For me, though, Red Rocks was about much more than a great musical spectacle. It was a turning point in my life and career. Never again would I be content to be a broadcaster; I was freed to follow my heart to be a musician.

Did I know immediately that the risk I was taking would pay off? No. Will you know immediately if the risk you're thinking about taking is going to pay off? Not likely. In fact, as you venture outside your comfort zone, don't be surprised if you feel disquieted, as though the walls of your stomach are about to cave in under the stress.

But don't let that stop you from stepping out of the normal, the ordinary, to take a risk that could change your future in ways you have never dreamed. A risk that could make your heart beat anew and bring more fulfillment than you have ever dared to consider.

How do you know if the time is right to take that risk? Lay your heart on the line. Ask God to help you do something great, something important, something beautiful, something of eternal value. Then dare to make it happen. And believe anything is possible.

Life is either a daring adventure or nothing.

—

HELEN KELLER

[Dare to be fulfilled.]

The people who get on in this world are the people who get up and look
for the circumstances they want and if they can't find them, make them.

—

GEORGE BERNARD SHAW

[True fulfillment lies in
God's purpose for you.]

LEGACY

Make your now wow, your minutes miracles, and your days pay.
Your life will have been magnificently lived and invested,
and when you die you will have made a difference.

—

MARK VICTOR HANSEN

The plans of the Lord stand firm forever,
the purposes of his heart through all generations.

—

PSALM 33:11 NIV

All of us leave our mark on the world, whether we lived meaningfully or ineffectively. The remarkable thing about a legacy is that each of us gets to decide what ours will be. Those who have made a great impact have lived the belief that their dreams were worth risking lesser things. Effective living demands passion and purpose, courage and faith.

Passion is infectious. It is also an essential ingredient of motivation to change circumstances. And the energy it exudes draws others into the vision, modeling health and vitality for future generations to observe and carry on.

A person is never too old to affect his own legacy.

Twelve million viewers watched me every evening on *Entertainment Tonight,* and to them I was the guy who read the birthdays. They were never going to go for John Tesh, the singer. But I had to be true to my heart's calling; I had to figure out what legacy I wanted to leave in the world. And then I had to figure out how to get the wheels rolling.

I had no idea what that first Red Rocks venture would lead to. But I dreamed, hoped, prayed, and acted. And those actions paid off in amazing and unexpected ways. The second trip to Red Rocks signified the developing legacy that had been birthed years earlier. Yes, there were labor pains along the way. But that's true of any worthwhile endeavor.

My prayer now is for God's continued guidance and for his hand on the pulse of this dream that he brought to fruition. Without him it simply would not be.

May the legacy live on. . . .

Future generations will recall something about you. Imagine what you will be remembered for when your days on earth are done. You have daily opportunities to contribute to your legacy. Viewing each moment as an investment in the future raises the stakes on the choices you make and how you prioritize your time.

The first step to leaving a powerful legacy is to take seriously the dreams of your heart. That means encouraging your dreams to soar. It means diving in to life and pushing beyond your perceived capabilities. And it means looking to God for guidance and help.

None of us know how much time we have on earth. At the end of your life, will your thoughts be full of If onlys? Or will your final breath be peaceful and free of regret for what might have been?

Your life will count for something. Make it good.

The key is in not spending time, but in investing it.

—

STEPHEN R. COVEY

[Leave something behind.]

There are only two lasting bequests we can hope to give our children. One
of these is roots . . . the other, wings.

—

HENRY WARD BEECHER

[You were created to make a difference.]

92

A FINAL NOTE

Will I continue to do concerts? I'd like to think so. As long as people want to attend the concerts, I will continue to perform them. Whatever I do, I want to do it with passion, a sense of adventure, and a pure love for God, who created every one of us to make a difference in the world.

I have lived and will continue to live each day risking it all. Every talent I have falls under the category of "God did this." Knowingly or unwittingly, I have allowed myself to be open to what he was doing in my life. He has taken me on this amazing ride and has shown me again and again that to believe in his unconditional love is the greatest—and ironically, the safest—risk of all. Consequently, I have allowed myself to risk and even fail often. Things might not have worked out so well if I hadn't worked hard, loved hard, and lived with passion. All I can tell you is that I have grabbed all of life that I can get, and it's been good. Along the way I have made some bad choices, too, but God has worked it all for good.

He will do the same for you. If you will simply trust God with your future and take each step of obedience as he leads you, he will guide you on a tremendously exciting journey. And remember, his dreams for you are infinitely more incredible than your own dreams for you!

"For I know the plans I have for you," says the Lord. "They are plans for good and not for disaster, to give you a future and a hope."

—

JEREMIAH 29:11